Wolf Pack

Wolf Pack
Tracking Wolves in the Wild

Sylvia A. Johnson
&
Alice Aamodt

· LERNER PUBLICATIONS COMPANY ·
MINNEAPOLIS

This book is available in two editions:
Library binding by Lerner Publications Company
Soft cover by First Avenue Editions
241 First Avenue North
Minneapolis, Minnesota 55401

Library of Congress Cataloging in Publication Data

Johnson, Sylvia A.
  Wolf pack.

  Includes index.
  Summary: Describes the social interaction of wolves in a pack
as they share the work of hunting, maintaining territory, and
raising young.
  1. Wolves—Juvenile literature. [1. Wolves] I. Aamodt, Alice.
II. Title.
QL737.C22J65   1985   599.74'442   85-37
ISBN 0-8225-1577-6 (lib. bdg.)
ISBN 0-8225-9526-5 (pbk.)

10 – P/JR – 02 00 99 98 97 96 95 94

Contents

Introduction

THE TRACKS IN THE CRUSTY SNOW ARE DEEP AND WIDE. They look like the footprints of a large, heavy dog—a husky, perhaps, or a Great Dane. The marks made by the round pads and the sharp claws of the animal's feet can be seen clearly in the slanting light of the late afternoon sun. Placed neatly one behind the other, the tracks cross the clearing in a straight line and disappear into the deep shadows of the pine forest.

Behind the first set of tracks are the footprints of several other four-footed travelers. They are similar in form to the marks made by the lead animal, but most are smaller. These tracks too move in neat, straight lines over the snow-covered ground. They seem to be made by animals traveling swiftly over familiar territory, creatures confident and at home in the cold northern forest.

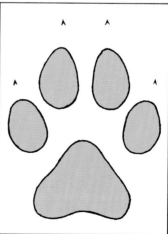

At one time, tracks like these could be found in many parts of the world. Throughout the continents of the Northern Hemisphere—Europe, North America, Asia—they appeared in forests and plains, in isolated wilderness areas and close to human settlements. Today few people will ever see these impressive prints or the animal that makes them.

The track of the wolf has become a rare sight in the modern world, and the animal's distinctive voice is a sound seldom heard. But in some remote regions, the big footprints can still be found in winter snow or spring mud, and choruses of howls ring out through the quiet night. Despite human efforts to eradicate them, wolves still live on the earth.

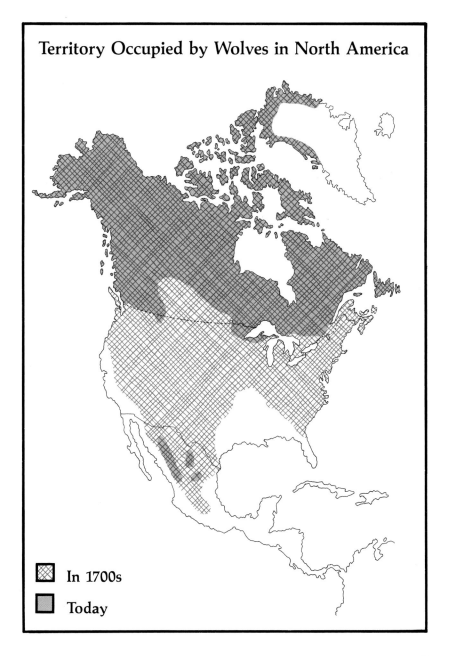

Territory Occupied by Wolves in North America

In 1700s

Today

·1·

What Is a Wolf?

I F YOU ARE LUCKY ENOUGH TO BE IN AN AREA WHERE wolves live and to see wolf tracks, you will immediately notice how much they look like the footprints of a large dog. The wolf is in fact a wild dog, a member of the scientific family Canidae, which includes domestic dogs as well as other doglike wild animals such as foxes and jackals.

Scientists believe that wolves are the direct ancestors of today's domestic dogs. They think that early humans domesticated wild wolves to make them useful companions and work animals. Since that time, selective breeding has produced the many varieties of domestic dogs, some of which are very unwolf-like in appearance and habit.

Despite these differences, it is clear that wolves and dogs still have many things in common. In appearance, a wolf closely resembles a husky or malamute dog, except that it is larger, with longer legs and bigger feet. The

Like the wolf, the jackal is a wild dog, a member
of the scientific family Canidae.

average male wolf weighs between 70 and 100 pounds (about
32 to 45 kilograms) and measures 5 to 6.5 feet (1.5 to
1.9 meters) from the tip of its nose to the end of its bushy
tail. Female wolves are usually smaller, with an average
weight of 55 to 90 pounds (about 24 to 41 kilograms) and
a length of 4.5 to 6 feet (1.3 to 1.8 meters).

In the canid family, domestic dogs are noted for their
variety of shapes, sizes, and colors. Although there is only
one species of domestic dog, *Canis familiaris*, there are more
than 120 breeds as different from each other as the tiny,
almost hairless chihuahua and the massive, shaggy St.
Bernard. Wolves too make up a single species, *Canis lupus*,
that includes some variations, although nothing like the
differences that breeding has produced in the domestic dog.

All wolves have the same basic body structure, but they vary considerably in their coloring. The majority of wolves are some shade of gray; in fact, *Canis lupus* is often commonly called the gray wolf. The gray coloring is produced by a blend of various colors—white, black, chestnut, gray—in the long *guard hairs* of a wolf's coat, or *pelage.* Gray-coated wolves usually have black-tipped hairs across their shoulders and a band of black down their backs and tails.

Some "gray" wolves are not gray at all but have coats

Although these two wolf pups were born in the same litter, their coloring is quite different.

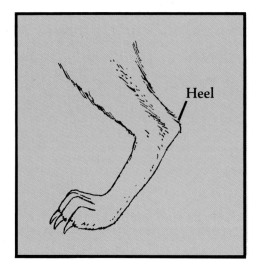

Heel

A canid's heel is positioned high up on the leg. When the animal runs, only the toes touch the ground.

that are cream-colored, white, or black. These different *color phases* are found in the same areas where populations of gray-coated gray wolves are living. The black and white wolves are born with their distinctively colored coats, often to parents whose pelage is the more ordinary gray. They usually keep their colors throughout their lives, except that black wolves sometimes become gray with age just as humans do.

Like domestic dogs and all other canids, wolves have 42 teeth, 20 in the upper jaw and 22 in the lower. A wolf's 4 canine teeth or fangs are particularly conspicuous, often measuring 2.5 inches (6.25 centimeters) from root to tip. These long, slightly curved teeth enable a wolf to get a good grip on its prey and hold on until the animal is brought down. Its other teeth—incisors, premolars, and molars—are useful for cutting, scraping, and grinding food.

Another characteristic that the wolf shares with fellow members of the dog clan is its method of moving on its toes.

The graceful, quick-moving collie is a typical
member of the family Canidae.

Unlike humans, canids keep the back parts of their feet
raised when they walk or run. This method of locomotion,
called *digitigrade* movement, is used by horses and cats as
well as dogs, all animals whose ways of life often depend
on swift, silent motion. Humans, apes, monkeys, and bears
use *plantigrade* movement, putting their feet flat on the ground
with each step. Such flat-footed creatures do not move with
the grace and speed of wolves and other digitigrade animals.

In addition to many features of their appearance and
physical makeup, there are other characteristics that wolves
share with dogs: keen senses of smell and hearing, the habit
of panting to keep cool. Wolves also differ from dogs in
some important ways: they breed (mate and produce young)

only once a year, whereas domestic dogs are capable of breeding twice during a single year; their legs move in a different way when running.

Of all the similarities and differences between dogs and wolves, however, some of the most interesting have nothing to do with physical characteristics. Instead, they are in the more intangible area of social behavior—how the animals live with others of their kind and how they behave in relation to other creatures.

Domestic dogs are famous for their friendliness, for their warm and outgoing natures. Unlike the aloof cat, a pet dog

Descended from wolves like all domestic dogs, these Pekinese have inherited the outgoing social nature of their wolfish ancestors.

openly expresses affection for its human owners and for other animals with which it lives. Dogs are also known for the strong attachments they form and for their unwavering loyalty to their companions, both human and non-human.

Wolves, with their reputation for ferocity and cruelty, would hardly be expected to share these appealing characteristics. Yet the more we know about wolves, the more obvious it becomes that the animals have the same strong social nature that dogs have. They too form deep attachments to their companions—usually fellow wolves but sometimes humans or other animals. Wolves too have many ways of expressing their feelings for others, and such demonstrations are an important part of their lives. And if loyalty includes an instinct to work for the well-being and safety of other individuals, then wolves are among the most "loyal" members of the animal kingdom.

If wolves have these characteristics that humans find so attractive in their pet dogs, then why are the wild canids so despised and feared by most people? Part of the reason is that wolves are *predators*, hunters that kill other animals for their food. Human beings are also meat-eating predators, but most humans don't have to kill to get their own food, and they are repelled by animals that use their teeth and claws to obtain meat instead of buying it at the supermarket.

An even more important reason for the human dislike of wolves is ignorance of what the animals are really like. For centuries, popular legends about the wickedness and ferociousness of wolves (which come from a period in human history when people and wolves were rivals for food) have taken the place of real knowledge of the wolf's nature and habits. Today, the research of modern scientists has revealed to us the real wolf in all its complexity. There is no excuse for believing anymore in the "big, bad wolf" and its fearsome relatives.

·2·
Wolf Pack

A Family Group

I F YOU ARE LUCKY ENOUGH TO SEE WOLF TRACKS IN THE wild, you will probably not see the footprints of a single animal. Wolves travel in groups; they hunt in groups, and they perform almost all the other activities of their lives in the company of fellow wolves. This is one of the most important facts that modern science has learned about wolves and one of the things that most clearly explains their way of life.

The *pack*, the basic unit of wolf social life, is usually a family group. It is made up of animals related to each other by blood and family ties of affection and mutual aid. The core of a pack is a mated pair of wolves—an adult male and female that have bred and produced young. The other members of the pack are their offspring: young wolves ranging in age from pups to two- and three-year-olds. Most packs have 6 or 7 members, although some may include as many as 15 wolves.

Like members of all families, the individual wolves in a pack play different roles in relation to the others in the group. Just as in a human family, the parent wolves are the leaders of the pack. Scientists refer to them as the *alpha male* and *alpha female* to indicate their superior position within the *dominance hierarchy*, or pack social structure. (Alpha is the first letter in the Greek alphabet.)

The alpha male and female are the oldest members of the pack and the ones with the most experience in hunting, defending territory, and other important group activities. The other pack members respect their positions and follow their leadership in almost all things. The alpha wolves are usually the ones to make decisions for the pack, for instance, when the group should go out to hunt or move from one place to another.

The other pack members all have positions in the hierarchy inferior to those of the alpha male and female. The young adult wolves, who are the grown-up offspring of the alpha pair, have their own special roles under the leadership of their parents. Some of them are able to "boss around," or dominate, their sisters and brothers because they have established themselves as superior in some way. This superiority might be physical—larger size or greater strength—but it can also be based on personality. *Dominant* wolves in the pack usually have more aggressive and forceful personalities than their relatives of the same age.

The juveniles and pups—wolves under two years old—do not occupy permanent positions within the pack hierarchy. They all take orders from their parents and older brothers and sisters, but their relationships with each other change frequently. During their play and other activities, they are constantly testing one another to find out who will eventually be "top wolf" in their age group.

A wolf pack is a family group made up of parents
and their offspring of various ages.

Relationships among creatures that live close together in groups are often very complicated, and this is true of the ties that connect the members of a wolf pack. Scientific studies of captive wolves and wolf packs in the wild have shown that many complex rules of behavior seem to govern the way that the animals relate to each other. The methods that wolves use to communicate with fellow pack members are also quite elaborate.

Later chapters in this book will describe some of the fascinating details of wolf social behavior. As an introduction to the subject, however, we will take a look at the way in which newborn wolves become part of a pack and establish relationships with its older members.

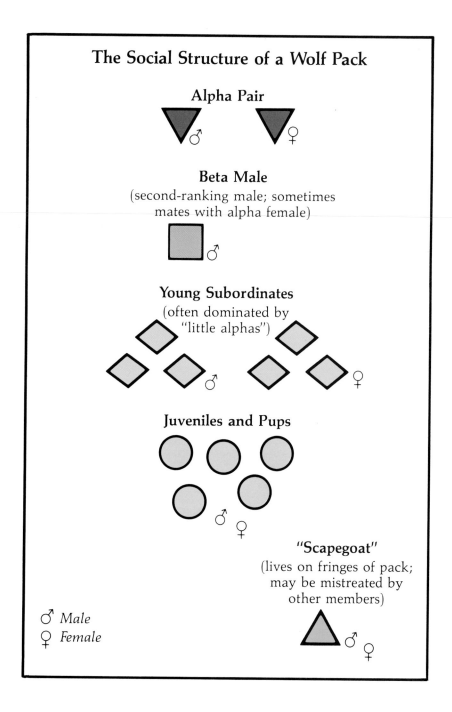

The Social Structure of a Wolf Pack

Alpha Pair

♂ ♀

Beta Male
(second-ranking male; sometimes
mates with alpha female)

♂

Young Subordinates
(often dominated by
"little alphas")

♂ ♀

Juveniles and Pups

♂ ♀

"Scapegoat"
(lives on fringes of pack;
may be mistreated by
other members)

♂ ♀

♂ Male
♀ Female

·3·

Wolf Pack

Pups Are Born

T HE ADDITION OF NEW MEMBERS IS AN IMPORTANT event in any family group, and a wolf pack is no exception to this rule. The birth of wolf pups affects all the members of the pack. They share in preparing for their arrival and in caring for the pups as they grow. Like other activities of the pack, the raising of young is a group effort.

Although all the members of the pack help to care for pups, just one pair of wolves usually gives birth to new offspring. In most packs, only the alpha male and female mate and reproduce. Even though there may be other wolves in the group old enough to produce young, they do not usually mate. The alpha pair uses their dominance over the other wolves to discourage them from mating. Sometimes they will use physical force to keep inferior pack members from forming pairs and mating.

The alpha female in the pack is almost always the mother of new wolf pups, but in some packs, the alpha male is not the father. For some reason, the male may not be interested in mating with the alpha female or with any other pack member. In this situation, his role is often taken over by another male wolf that scientists call the *beta male*. The beta male has a position in the pack hierarchy just under the alpha pair. This high-ranking wolf will mate with the alpha female so that the pack may produce new members.

Like most animals, female wolves are in *heat*—that is, capable of mating and producing young—for only a few weeks during the year. The mating season occurs at the end of winter so that the wolf pups will have time to develop and grow strong before next winter's cold and snow come to the northern lands where most wolves live. In some areas, wolves may mate as early as January, while in the far north— for example, Alaska and northern Canada—mating may take place as late as April.

When the mating season arrives, all the members of the wolf pack are aware that something important is about to happen. There is a sense of excitement in the pack and a period of increased activity as the wolves prepare for this event in the yearly cycle of their lives. The alpha pair in particular begins to exhibit a different pattern of behavior.

While the alpha male and female have a close relationship throughout the year, during the mating season, they are especially affectionate. They stay close to each other most of the time, even while sleeping, and frequently rub their bodies and heads together. During this period of *courtship*, they reaffirm the ties that bind them to each other and get ready for the act of mating.

During the period of courtship, the alpha male and female are constant and loving companions.

The courtship and mating of the alpha pair are not
private events in a wolf pack. All pack members
are witnesses of these important activities.

Mating may take place several times between the alpha pair (or between the alpha female and the beta male) before the female's period of heat is over. These unions usually result in the conception of new life and the birth of wolf pups about nine weeks later.

A few weeks before her pups are to be born, the pregnant female begins preparing a home for her new family. She selects a *den* that will serve as a secure shelter for the helpless pups. A wolf den can be created in many different spots: a rock cave, a hollow log, an old beaver house. The most common kind of den, however, is a burrow usually dug into the soft dirt or sand of a hillside. It has a small entrance just large enough for an adult wolf to get through. Connected to the entrance is a narrow tunnel that may extend for 10 feet (3 meters) or more. At the end of the tunnel is an enlarged chamber where the pups will be born and where they will spend the first weeks of their lives.

The entrance to a wolf den

The female wolf digs her den with her paws, piling up a mound of dirt at the entrance. In addition to making a new den, she will often clean out last year's den so that it is ready for use in an emergency, for instance, if the new den is flooded with water. If there is no soft dirt or sand available, a wolf will sometimes make a home for herself and her pups out of the abandoned den of another animal such as a fox.

While the female is busy preparing a den, other members of the pack are also making ready for the birth of the pups. The alpha male, the partner of the pregnant female, is at work storing food for her to eat during the time that she will stay in the den with the pups. He brings back pieces of meat from the animals killed in the hunt and buries them in *caches* near the dens. Other pack members may also help in storing food for the alpha female.

When the time for the birth is near, the female wolf enters the den alone. This is one job that she must do by herself.

Most female wolves give birth to 5 or 6 pups, although some *litters* contain as few as 2 or as many as 10. As each of her pups are born, the female licks it vigorously to break and remove the amniotic sac that surrounds the tiny animal. Then she bites through the umbilical cord, which served as the pup's lifeline while inside her body. After cleaning the youngster thoroughly with her tongue, she gently pushes it toward the nipples on her belly. Once the pup has found a nipple, it begins to suck instinctively, taking in the warm milk that will sustain its young life.

Like dog puppies, wolf pups are helpless at birth. They cannot see or hear, and they are unable to maintain their own body temperatures. Their average weight is only one pound (0.5 kilograms). For the first few weeks of their lives, they depend entirely on their mothers for food, warmth, and protection.

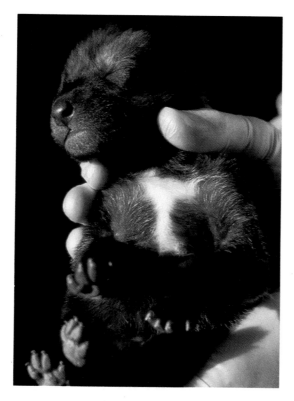

This tiny wolf pup is only a few days old.

During this time of early development, wolf pups do little but eat and sleep. Within the dark inner chamber of the den, they huddle close to their mother and their littermates, making high-pitched whining noises when they are hungry or cold. Even at this early stage, the individual personalities of the pups are beginning to show. Some may be more aggressive than others, pushing their brothers and sisters aside in their eagerness to nurse. When they grow up, these aggressive young wolves may become the dominant members of the pack, ruling over packmates as they now dominate their weaker or less forceful littermates.

The mother wolf is kept busy feeding and guarding her hungry offspring, but she periodically leaves the den to eat and drink herself. The cached food is nearby, and her mate often leaves pieces of fresh meat outside the den entrance as well. She also drinks large amounts of water from the lake or stream that is always located close to the den site. The female needs to be well-nourished so that she will have adequate milk to satisfy the rapidly growing pups.

Wolf pups do develop quickly, changing from helpless babies to active, inquisitive youngsters in four to five weeks. Within two weeks of their birth, their eyes open, although their keen sight will not develop completely for several months.

Two and a half weeks old, these wolf pups are still too young to leave the protection of the den.

At the end of these first two weeks, their baby, or milk, teeth begin to appear. When they are three weeks old, the pups are able to hear and to eat some solid food. They now weigh about seven pounds (3.2 kilograms) and can walk on all four legs instead of crawling on their stomachs as they did in the first weeks of their lives.

During this early period, the pups never leave the den. Their mother is the only member of the pack that has contact with them. When they are about one month old, however, they are ready to meet their other relatives for the first time.

The female wolf calls her pups from the entrance of the den, making the whimpering sound that adult wolves often use in communicating with their young. When the pups come tumbling out of the den, seeing the light of day for the first time, the other pack members hurry to greet their young relatives. The adult wolves sniff, nuzzle, and lick the pups, wagging their tails excitedly. They seem delighted by the new additions to the pack and eager to make their acquaintance.

After the pups leave the den for the first time, they become the responsibility of the whole pack. They are still being nursed by their mother, but the other pack members now share the job of protecting the pups as they explore the territory near the den. The older wolves all keep an eye on the curious youngsters and bring them back if they wander too far away. They also watch for predators like eagles and hawks that might swoop down and snatch the pups up in their claws. If such threats are detected, an adult hurries the pups into the protection of the den.

When the pups are ready to eat solid food, the pack members play an important role in supplying them with meat. The young wolves first reach this stage in their development when they are about three weeks of age. In addition to her milk, the mother wolf begins to give them partially digested meat that she has eaten. She *regurgitates* this semi-liquid food from her stomach onto the ground, and the pups devour it. After the pups leave the den, other members of the pack also frequently regurgitate food for them, sharing their prey with their young relatives who are not yet able to hunt for themselves.

The pups quickly learn that the older pack members are a source of food, and they begin soliciting meals from these four-legged kitchens. When the older wolves return from hunting, the pups rush to greet them, nibbling, nuzzling, and licking their mouths. This signal tells the adults that the pups are hungry (wolf pups are almost always hungry) and causes them to regurgitate some of the partially digested meat in their own stomachs. Most observers say that the older wolves seem eager to feed their young relatives and will give them food even without solicitation.

Along with eating, playing is one of the most important activities of a pup's life. Running, chasing, pouncing, fighting, chewing on everything in sight: young wolves spend almost all their waking hours on these exciting pastimes. Like most young animals, pups develop their bodies through play and also practice skills that will be important in their adult lives.

Although a pup's primary companions are its littermates, other members of the family also participate in the strenuous fun. Yearling wolves—last year's pups—may join their younger brothers and sisters in games of pounce and chase. Older pack members tolerantly allow themselves to be the targets of the pups' energetic attacks. Youngsters climb over the adults as they lie resting on the ground and vigorously nip at their ears and tails. Only when the play becomes too boisterous or goes on too long will an adult wolf get up and leave the pups or reprimand them by growling and baring its teeth.

Exploring in the grass
or wrestling with
littermates, a wolf
pup learns the skills
that it will need in
later life.

In play as in all their other activities, wolf pups are intimately involved with other members of the pack. This closeness creates bonds of affection and familiarity that will last for as long as they remain with the pack. Through their daily contact with the older pack members, pups learn to trust and depend on their companions. Through trial and error, they also learn about the pack hierarchy and about their own positions in it.

This period of intensive learning and establishing of relationships lasts for about 11 weeks. People who have cared for orphaned wolf pups during these early weeks have discovered that the young wolves learn to relate to their human caretakers just as they would to older members of a pack. The pups greet human companions affectionately and enthusiastically, engage them in boisterous play, and even try to solicit food from them by licking and nipping their mouths. As the pups grow older, they maintain these early ties with their human friends, accepting them as fellow pack members who walk on two legs instead of four.

Wolves taken into captivity after their first weeks of puppyhood, however, do not learn to relate to humans. Because the formative period of their development is over, they are shy and distrustful of strangers. Juvenile wolves in the wild react in the same way when confronted with any animals other than their packmates. After the first 11 weeks of their lives, young wolves know exactly who their friends are. Any creature outside the close-knit circle of the pack is either prey or a potential enemy to be feared and avoided.

HOW A WOLF PACK GROWS AND CHANGES

A new pack is usually formed by a male wolf and a female wolf who have left other packs and are living on their own. The wolves mate and produce young, who become the subordinate members of the new pack under the leadership of their parents, the alpha pair.

As the young wolves grow into adulthood, they assume different roles within the pack. Some become what scientists call *biders*. They stay in the pack, waiting for an opportunity to move up the hierarchy and take the alpha positions themselves. This may happen when the alpha wolves die or become too old and weak to act as leaders.

Other young wolves, often the more aggressive ones, are *dispersers*. They leave the pack and become *lone wolves*, wandering and hunting by themselves. If they can find mates and available territories, they will become the founders of new packs.

·4·

Wolf Pack

Keeping in Touch

WHEN WOLF PUPS ARE BORN INTO A PACK, ONE OF the most important things they must learn is the "language" of the group, the method by which pack members keep in touch with each other, sharing information and communicating their feelings. Scientists have discovered that wolves have a very complicated system of communication, quite different from the language of humans but used in a similar way to convey meaning.

An efficient system of communication is vital to all animals that live in groups. In order for the members of a pack, a family, or a nation to cooperate and to live peacefully together, there must be a way for individuals to let others know what they are planning and feeling. Human societies use words, both spoken and written, as a means of communication among their members. A wolf pack communicates with sounds, but it also employs smells, movements, and body positions to convey information of various kinds.

Because rank and hierarchy are so important to the orderly functioning of a wolf pack, much of the communication among pack members is related to this aspect of their lives. Using movements and body positions, the leaders of the pack continually remind the other wolves of their dominant roles in the group. In return, the subordinate wolves communicate their respect and affection for—and sometimes their fear of—the pack leaders.

One of the clearest symbols of a wolf's rank in a pack is the position of its tail. Unlike the tails of many breeds of dogs, a wolf's long, bushy tail normally hangs down rather than curling up over its back. The alpha wolves in a pack,

With its tail tucked between its legs, a low-ranking pack member (left) approaches an alpha wolf.

however, usually hold their tails high in the air instead of letting them droop.

In any pack, the wolf carrying its tail high like a hairy banner will almost always be the alpha male. The alpha female also holds her tail high, although usually not as high as that of her mate. Wolves occupying positions below the pack leaders keep their tails correspondingly low, especially in any confrontation with the alpha pair. The lowest-ranking members of the pack tuck their tails between their legs to express their inferiority to the wolves above them in the hierarchy.

The positions of other body parts are also used as a means of communicating status in the pack. An alpha wolf usually keeps its ears standing up, while low-ranking pack members lay their ears back. They also keep their fur flat, in contrast to the fluffed-out fur of the pack leaders.

There are some occasions in the life of the pack that call for more specific expressions of the relationships among the pack members. When a low-ranking wolf approaches one of the pack leaders, it keeps its body low to the ground, with its fur and ears flattened. From this position, it reaches up with its muzzle and gently licks or nips the muzzle of the alpha wolf. Sometimes all the pack members gather around the alpha male and greet him in this manner, often when he returns to the pack after being away for a while.

Scientists call this behavior *active submission* and see it as a method whereby the pack members express friendly feelings toward the leaders and respect for their authority. The gesture of licking and nipping a leader's muzzle is similar to the food-begging behavior of wolf pups and may be related to it. By using this gesture, the subordinate wolves seem to be saying to an alpha wolf: We depend on you and look up to you in the same way that pups depend on and look up to the adults that give them food and protection.

Pack members enthusiastically greet one of their leaders (left).

Sometimes the interaction between the dominant wolves and the rest of the pack is not so friendly. If an alpha feels that a pack member is resisting its authority, it may take strong measures to bring the rebellious wolf back in line. Often a stern and unwavering stare is enough to convince the rebel that it should submit itself to the pack leader. Like dogs and many other animals, wolves avoid looking each other directly in the eye unless they are trying to exert their authority.

An even stronger message of authority is given when a dominant wolf growls and bares its teeth at an inferior or crouches as if to spring on the offender. When a subordinate

A dominant wolf sometimes expresses its authority by growling and baring its teeth at an inferior.

**The wolf on the ground is making a gesture of
passive submission to the standing wolf.**

wolf is threatened in this way, it usually makes a gesture of
passive submission by lying on the ground and exposing its
side or belly to the threatener. This movement, which is also
performed by pups, seems to convey a message of helplessness
and dependence—"I'm harmless, please don't hurt me." Satisfied
by this admission of inferiority, the dominant wolf accepts
the rebel's "apology," and peace is restored in the pack.

44•

The main purpose of all the communications expressing rank and relationships within the pack is to keep peace. Pack members rarely fight with each other because they have so many other ways of settling their differences and establishing their proper positions in the group. Physical conflict, which would be destructive to the well-being of the pack, is avoided by the use of a language of gestures and symbolic actions.

Of course, not all the communications that take place in a pack have to do with such serious subjects. Frequently, the message that one pack member wants to convey to another is, "Let's play!"

This wolf is using body positions and movements to invite a fellow pack member to play.

Adult wolves, like pups, enjoy chasing, wrestling, and tumbling on the ground. When a wolf is looking for a play-mate, it may approach another wolf, bow down low with its front legs flat on the ground, and wag its tail vigorously. If the invitation is not accepted, it will be repeated and sometimes alternated with leaping about in a zigzag fashion. (Many dogs make almost exactly the same movements when they are in a playful mood.) If the other wolf is willing to play, the two will engage in mock fights or take turns chasing each other until both are worn out and ready to rest.

Invitations to play and messages about social status in the pack are usually conveyed by means of movements and postures, but wolves also use sounds to communicate with each other. The animals are capable of making several kinds of sounds, including the threatening growl or snarl and the whimper used in communications between pups and adults. The most famous wolf sound is, of course, the howl, and it is a very important part of wolf language.

When people think about howling, they usually imagine a mournful, lonely sound made by a wolf sitting all alone on a hilltop in the moonlight. Like most human images of wolves, however, this one is not very accurate. Wolves howl at any time, not just at night, and they often howl together, not alone.

Group or chorus howling is another means by which the members of a wolf pack reaffirm their ties with each other and their closeness as a group. One wolf—often the alpha male—will point its nose at the sky, open its mouth, and start to howl. Immediately the other members of the pack rush to stand beside him, shoulder to shoulder, and join their voices to his. The whole group seems to be excited and happy, tails wagging and bodies wiggling. Each wolf howls on its own note so that a grand chorus of slightly different sounds is produced.

The howl is a very important part of wolf "language."

Chorus howling often takes place before a wolf pack goes out to hunt. This ceremony of togetherness may encourage the pack members to cooperate with each other in the difficult job of finding and bringing down prey. At the end of a successful hunt, the pack may also celebrate with a group howl. While wolves are on the track of prey, they are usually silent.

There are occasions when a wolf will howl by itself. This may happen when an animal is separated from the pack and is trying to locate its companions. Pack members seem to recognize each other's voices and will keep responding to the howl of their wandering relative until the group is reunited.

Because howling is a sound that carries over a considerable distance, it is very useful in communications among separated members of a pack. Howling is also used when members of different packs have to get in touch with each other to relay information about their location and their intentions.

Wolves usually have other wolves as neighbors, and the way in which neighboring packs live side by side, competing for prey and territory, is another fascinating aspect of the wolf story.

·5·

Wolf Pack

Neighbors and Rivals

WOLVES SPEND MOST OF THEIR LIVES IN CLOSE CONtact with members of their own packs, but they also live in a larger world shared by other creatures. The forests and fields where they make their homes and earn a living are also home to beaver and rabbit, to fox, deer, and moose, to birds of many kinds, perhaps to humans, and usually to other wolves. In order to survive, a wolf pack must deal successfully with this larger world and its inhabitants.

The world that a wolf pack shares with other creatures is not as well-organized as the society within a pack, but it does have certain rules and laws of behavior. Many of these rules govern relationships among neighboring wolf packs and are based on the existence of *territories*, areas in which individual packs live and hunt.

Studies of wolves in the wild have shown that many packs have fairly specific geographical areas

that they consider their own and that they will defend against the intrusion of other wolves. A territory must be defended because it is the source of the pack's livelihood, the area that contains its food supply. Although the region may be home to many other kinds of creatures, it cannot be easily shared by other wolves, who would compete for the limited number of prey animals available.

The size of a pack's territory can vary from 10 square miles (26 square kilometers) per wolf to 500 square miles (1,300 square kilometers) for each pack member. Smaller territories exist in areas where prey animals are relatively abundant and where they stay in one place all year round. In North America, these conditions exist in the forests of Minnesota and southern Canada, and wolves living here tend to have smaller home territories with clearly defined boundaries.

Large territories are found in Alaska and other regions of the far north where prey is less available and where yearly migrations of prey animals are common. For example, the caribou that are the chief food supply of Alaskan wolves travel hundreds of miles each year between their summer and winter homes. Under such conditions, wolves must follow their prey and hunt over extremely large areas. The boundaries of their territories are vague and difficult to define.

In areas where territorial boundaries are distinct and important, members of a wolf pack must let other wolves know just where these lines are located. Although the animals cannot post written signs saying "Keep Out!", they can convey the same unmistakable message in their own way.

One of the most important methods that wolves use to indicate their territories is *scent marking*. Like domestic dogs and other canids, wolves have keen senses of smell and are able to learn a great deal about their environment by picking up odors left by other creatures. When pack members want

An alpha wolf leaves a scent mark.

to tell other wolves about the location of their territory, they make use of a very powerful scent messenger: urine.

Members of a pack are apparently able to identify the distinctive odors of their packmates' urine, and they can also recognize the urine of strange wolves. To indicate the area of their territory, pack members mark it generously with the strong-smelling liquid. Other packs venturing into the region will discover these signs of prior ownership and leave quietly or risk a fight.

Scent marking by urination has its own special rules and methods. Instead of urinating on the ground, as would be common in ordinary urination, the scent-marking wolf usually squirts a small amount of urine on a *scent post*, a raised object like a tree stump or a rock. The animal accomplishes this by raising one of its hind legs to urinate instead of squatting as wolves normally do. (Male dogs mark their "territories" in just the same manner.)

Scientists studying wolves have discovered that this *raised-leg urination*—RLU, for short—is usually performed only by the high-ranking wolves in the pack hierarchy, particularly the alpha male. The alpha female also marks with RLUs, often on a scent post that has just been marked by her mate. All other females in the pack, as well as the low-ranking males and the pups, usually urinate in a squatting position. These SQUs are not as important in marking territory as the RLUs of the dominant wolves.

When a wolf pack is moving on its daily rounds through its territory, the high-ranking wolves leave RLUs about every 500 yards (about 350 meters). They mark particularly heavily near the boundaries of the territory, where it borders the territories of other packs. Scent posts in these regions may be marked over and over again, leaving very strong evidence that the pack is in possession.

If wolves from neighboring packs cross these scent-marked boundaries and are discovered by the territory's occupants, they may be in for a lot of trouble. At the least, the invaders may be chased out of the area. If they don't run fast enough, they may be attacked and injured or killed by pack members defending their home territory. On some occasions, however, a large pack may enter the territory of a smaller pack and drive out the rightful owners by virtue of their greater numbers and strength.

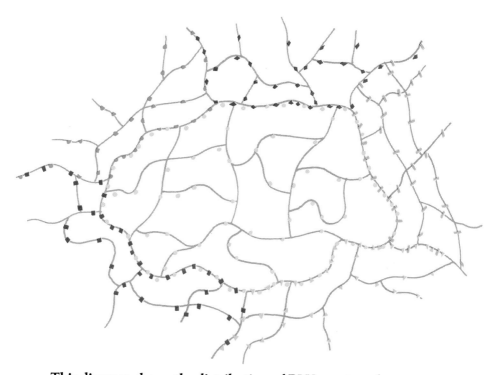

This diagram shows the distribution of RLU scent marks in the territory of one wolf pack (blue circles) and in the adjacent territories of several other packs (other colors). As you can see, all the packs mark more heavily around the borders of their territories than they do along the routes within them.

Scent marking is a very practical way for members of a pack to communicate to other wolves the extent and boundaries of their territory. It produces not only a physical signpost but also a kind of time clock that records the pack's movements. If scent marks around a territory are several weeks old, outsiders might assume that the territory's owners are not in residence at the moment and that it would be safe to venture into the area in pursuit of prey. This reading of the time element in the signs allows greater flexibility in the use of available territories and at the same time avoids confrontations between rival packs.

By howling, wolves can let members of other packs know their whereabouts and warn them against trespassing.

Howling is a means of immediate communication between packs, a method by which one group of wolves can tell another, "We are here in our territory, and we will put up with no interference from outsiders." Wolves do advertise their presence in this way, answering the howls of a neighboring pack with their own ringing chorus. On some occasions, however, pack members seem to feel that silence affords better protection than a noisy howl.

For example, when a pack has young pups, howling near the den is kept to a minimum. The pups are vulnerable, and attracting attention to their whereabouts might be dangerous. On the other hand, if a pack of adult wolves has made a kill in its territory and eaten only part of the animal, the wolves will probably howl loudly at the kill site. This will let other wolves know that they are still enjoying their feast and not about to give any of it up to outsiders. When the prey has been reduced to a few bones and some hair, it is not worth howling about and the pack will be silent. Often, it will not even answer if it hears a challenging howl from another pack.

By means of howling, scent marking, and other methods of communication, neighboring packs keep in touch and generally succeed in staying out of each other's way. Avoiding conflict is to everyone's advantage, unless extreme situations —for instance, a shortage of prey—make it necessary for a pack to violate the rules in order to survive.

Survival is the ultimate goal of every wolf pack, and an adequate supply of food is essential to achieving that goal. Securing food is probably the most important activity in the life of a pack. It is also the one that most often brings wolves into conflict with other wolves and with predators even more dangerous—human beings.

·6·

Wolf Pack

Killing to Survive

E VEN UNDER NORMAL CIRCUMSTANCES, SURVIVAL IS NOT easy for wolves in the wild. Their lives as predators are difficult, and they often go hungry for days, even weeks, at a time. Although wolves are skillful hunters, they face many obstacles in their search for prey. Only their ability to act as a group makes it possible for them to feed themselves and their young.

Wolves are *carnivores*, or meat-eaters, and hunting is a year-round activity for a wolf pack. In winter snow or summer heat, pack members must search for the prey animals on which their diet depends. A pack's hunting schedule varies somewhat, however, depending on the time of year.

During the spring and summer, all the pack's activities are controlled by the presence of the pups and the need to guard and care for them. For the few weeks that the pups are in the den with the mother wolf, the other pack members go out to hunt, usually at night, and return to the den site the next day.

When the pups are 8 to 10 weeks old and able to leave the den, they are moved to a *rendezvous site* within the pack's territory. A rendezvous site is just what the name suggests; it is a meeting place for pack members as well as a home base for the pups. While their relatives are out on their nightly round of hunting, the pups stay at the site with an adult "pupsitter." The hunters return each morning with food for the young and then spend the day resting or playing at the rendezvous site. A pack usually uses one site for two or three weeks before moving the pups to a different spot, probably to be closer to prey animals.

A "pupsitter" watches over the young members of the pack.

The autumn and winter schedule of a wolf pack is quite different. By this time of year, the pups are at least six months old and capable of traveling with the adult wolves, although at a somewhat slower pace. Now the pack is on the move day and night, stopping only for periods of rest, play, and feeding. The group has no permanent or even semi-permanent head-quarters but rambles throughout its territory, following the trails of the animals on which it preys.

Just what these prey animals are depends on the part of the world in which the pack lives. In general, however, most wolves hunt hooved mammals like moose, deer, caribou, elk, and mountain sheep. Wolves are able to take these large animals because they hunt in groups, combining their strength and cunning to catch and kill their prey. A wolf hunting alone is able to capture animals like beavers, rabbits, hares, mice, and birds. Most of these smaller creatures, however, make only a mouthful for a hungry wolf. In order to feed its many members, a pack must be able to bring down large prey.

Locating prey is the first big job of hunting wolves. During their daily or nightly travels, the predators are always alert for signs that prey animals are nearby. Most frequently, the signs are in the form of scents picked up from the air by the wolves' sensitive noses. If the wind is blowing from the direction of the prey animals toward the wolves, the predators are able to smell the odor as much as a mile and a half away. Wolves can also use their sense of smell to follow the fresh tracks of animals on the ground, although wind-borne odors more often lead them to their prey.

When a pack of wolves picks up the scent of prey, the animals become very excited and alert. They sniff the air and then set off in the direction of their quarry, moving swiftly but cautiously. Their goal is to get close to the prey without revealing their presence, so silence and speed are essential.

The alpha wolves are first in line when the pack is
hunting or feeding on prey.

If they succeed in their quest, the wolves dash toward the animal, surround it, and bring it down by biting its rump, sides, neck, and head. In most cases, death comes quickly, and the predators begin to tear at the prey's flesh with their strong teeth, pulling off large pieces and bolting them down with very little chewing. By the time they are done, nothing will be left of the animal but the stomach contents (the remains of plant food, not to the taste of these meat-eaters), hooves, and perhaps some of the largest bones. The wolves eat everything else.

If the prey animals pick up the scent of the wolves or see them approaching, then the hunt may have a different outcome. The animals may escape by running, or they may stand and try to defend themselves against the predators' attack. Both methods have saved many potential prey from becoming a meal for a wolf pack.

Deer and caribou, which are also members of the deer family, are swift runners and, given half a chance, can escape from a pursuing wolf pack. The larger, heavier moose is not so fleet, but with a headstart, it can also get away from the predators. Wolves will chase a running animal for only so long. If they cannot quickly close the gap between themselves and their prey, they will usually give up the chase and look for an easier quarry. Wolves are very practical predators, and they seem to have a good sense of how much energy they should expend in pursuing prey. If the exertion of a long-distance chase would take more energy than would be gained from eating the object of the chase, then it is not worth the effort.

Hunting wolves can also be thwarted by a prey animal that puts up a vigorous self-defense. Moose are particularly successful in using this method of escape. If an adult moose is pursued by a wolf pack, it will sometimes stand and face its attackers instead of running. A full-grown male moose weighs

**An adult moose can often fight off a wolf attack,
but moose calves are unable to defend themselves.**

as much as 1,250 pounds (about 560 kilograms) and has a
massive set of antlers on its head. In defending itself, a moose
will try to gore an attacking wolf with its antlers or kick
the predator with its heavy hooves. Faced with this kind of
resistance, wolves will often give up the attack.

Because prey animals have so many avenues of escape,
wolves do not have a very high success rate in their careers
as hunters. Observers have estimated that less than 10 percent
of a pack's attempts to catch prey end successfully.

Wolves and Moose:
Hungry Predators versus Elusive Prey

This diagram shows the outcome of a wolf pack's encounters with moose. It is based on 68 hours of scientific observation that took place over three winters in Isle Royale National Park, located on an island in Lake Superior.

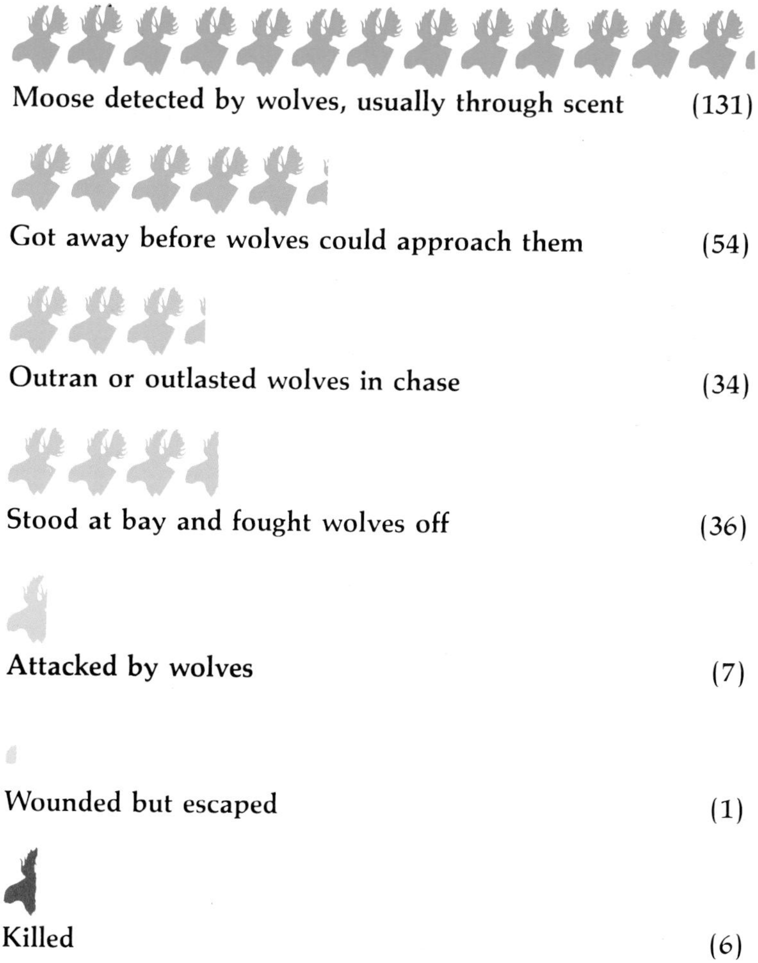

Moose detected by wolves, usually through scent   (131)

Got away before wolves could approach them   (54)

Outran or outlasted wolves in chase   (34)

Stood at bay and fought wolves off   (36)

Attacked by wolves   (7)

Wounded but escaped   (1)

Killed   (6)

Each figure represents 10 moose.

Luckily, wolves have a great capacity to go without food for long periods of time. They can survive for as much as two weeks without eating. When food is available, they gorge themselves to make up for the periods of famine. Adult wolves are capable of eating as much as 20 pounds (about 14 kilograms) of meat at one time.

When wolves are successful in taking prey, the animals they kill are usually not mature, healthy adults. Adult deer, caribou, and moose in good condition are able to escape the predators in most situations by fleeing or defending themselves. The animals that cannot escape are usually the very young, the old, and the diseased.

Young deer, moose, and caribou are not able to run as quickly as the adults, and they are incapable of defending themselves. During the spring and summer, a wolf pack's diet is made up largely of deer fawns or moose and caribou calves whose mothers have not been able to protect them from the predators' attacks.

At other times of the year, when there is not such a large supply of young prey, wolves seem to concentrate on the old and sick. Weakened by age or by the ravages of diseases and parasites, these animals too do not have the strength and speed needed to avoid the predators' sharp teeth.

From the human point of view, it might seem "unfair" of wolves to take advantage of their prey's weakness in this way. Of course, human standards of fairness have no meaning in the natural world. Wolves must have food in order to live, and they get it in the way that is easiest for them, expending the least amount of energy and producing the greatest return.

From this point of view, killing and eating young, old, and sick prey animals makes a great deal of sense. Surprisingly enough, it usually makes sense in terms of the prey's welfare too, at least when the group rather than the individual is considered. If wolves kill the old and sick caribou in a herd, then the younger, healthier members of the group will have more food, less chance of catching diseases, and a better chance of surviving. The health of the group will also be improved because these unfit animals will not be able to produce offspring that might inherit their unhealthy condition.

But what about wolves killing the young? How could that seemingly heartless slaughter benefit a group of prey animals? In many situations, it does just that by controlling the size of the prey population in a particular area. A smaller population means more food for survivors and, again, better health and living conditions for the group as a whole.

By killing young animals like this caribou calf (right), wolves act as a control on prey populations.

Of course, the relationship between wolves and their prey is not often so simple. Its delicate balance can be affected by many different factors, including human interference.

For example, in areas where the natural food supply of deer or moose has been damaged by severe weather or by human activities, populations of these plant-eating creatures will gradually decline. If wolves live in the area, they may bring about a further decline by preying on the remaining animals. This combination of destructive factors could eventually reduce the population drastically, perhaps to the point where the deer or moose are eliminated from the region. If this happens, the wolves too will be affected since their survival depends on an adequate supply of prey animals.

When the animals they prey on are gone, wolves either have to leave the area or look for another source of food. Sometimes they find an alternate source in the form of domestic animals—cattle, sheep, and other creatures confined on farms and ranches. If wild prey is not available, wolves will attack and kill domestic animals. The predators must have meat to survive, and of course, they do not recognize the fact that such animals are the property of human beings.

When wolves attack domestic animals, they sometimes behave differently than they do when killing wild prey. In the wild, wolves normally kill only what they need for food and they eat almost all of a prey animal. When domestic creatures are on the menu, however, the predators may kill many more animals than they can eat. They may consume only small portions of their prey and leave the carcasses almost untouched.

This "overkill" happens most frequently when wolves attack a large number of animals confined in a pen or a fenced area. Other predators such as wild cats also exhibit the same behavior in similar situations. Scientists believe that such abnormal behavior is produced by a kind of "short-circuit" in the predators' hunting instincts.

In the wild, killing is part of a whole set of instinctive actions that include searching for the prey, stalking and chasing it, and finally bringing it down and eating it. When predators are confronted by a group of domestic animals unable to run or to defend themselves, they are stimulated to perform only one part of the hunting sequence—the kill. They may kill again and again because the prey is available in large numbers and easy to catch, a situation that rarely exists in a natural setting.

Farmers and ranchers are understandably upset when wolves attack their animals in this way. In this situation as in so many others, however, the wolves are blamed for a problem that they did not create, a problem that exists because human activities have interfered with the predators' natural way of life. Such blame has frequently been part of the human attitude toward wolves. The troubled relationship between wolves and people has a very long history, most of which does little credit to the understanding or good sense of the human race.

·7·

Wolf Pack

Beasts of Myth and History

WOLVES AND HUMANS HAVE BEEN CROSSING EACH other's paths for many centuries, and the relationship between the two species of animals has been long and complex. In some times and places, wolves have been honored and respected by people, while in others, they have been despised and persecuted. A few groups of humans have considered the wolf their brother and equal, but many other human societies have seen the animal as an enemy of unsurpassed evil.

Throughout all these changes, the wolf's attitude toward people seems to have remained the same: fear and a healthy respect for fellow predators who are on the winning side of a very unequal battle for survival.

In the very early periods of human existence, there was probably little real conflict between wolves and people. During the great Ice Ages, small bands of humans

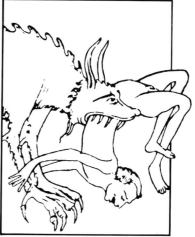

roamed the glacier-free lands of the Northern Hemisphere, following the grazing animals on which their livelihood depended. Wolves in large numbers also inhabited these areas. In this early period, both humans and wolves were wandering hunters, sometimes seeking the same kind of prey. The hunting ground was so vast and rich and people were so few in number, however, that serious competition was unlikely between the two groups of predators. Wolves and humans probably lived in a state of coexistence and mutual tolerance.

We have no way of knowing what attitudes prehistoric people held toward wolves, but we can get some idea by looking at the attitudes of nomadic hunters who have lived in historic times. The Plains Indians of North America shared their hunting territories with wolves and respected the skill and strength of these fellow predators. Indian hunters watched the way in which wolves moved quietly among the great herds of American bison (buffalo), seeking the most likely prey. In their own hunting of bison, they imitated the wolves' technique, even disguising themselves with wolf skins when they approached the giant animals.

Wolves not only served as models for hunting but they also played a significant role in the religious lives of the Plains tribes and other groups of North American Indians. The powerful and courageous predators were seen as representatives of important natural forces or spirits. Images of wolves often appeared in religious ceremonies, and some Indian healers included wolf skins in their medicine bundles, the collections of sacred materials that they used for curing illness.

Other Native American hunters who have known the wolf intimately are the Eskimos. Today as in the past, groups of Eskimos share their homeland on the cold northern tundra with wolf packs, hunting the same prey and leading the same kind of nomadic life.

Left: The Makah tribe of the American Northwest Coast used this wolf headdress in dance ceremonies.

Below: Artist George Catlin portrays the way in which Plains Indians disguised themselves as wolves when hunting bison.

Like the Indians of earlier times, Eskimos respect the wolf for its skill as a predator. They also admire the wolf's dedication to the welfare of its companions, a model of social behavior for humans and animals in the harsh Arctic environment. Eskimos, like Indians, sometimes kill wolves for their skins or for other specific reasons, but they believe that they are taking the life of an equal, not slaughtering a hated enemy.

Such coexistence between wolves and humans is possible only when there is no conflict between their ways of life. Conflict quickly arises when humans give up the nomadic life, settle down, and begin to produce their own food instead of hunting wild animals and gathering wild plants. Wolves have no choice but to continue their predatory way of life, but now they may find their prey not only among wild animals but also in the herds of sheep and cattle that people have

A scene on a decorated box shows ancient Sumerians herding a cow and three sheep. When early people like the Sumerians first domesticated animals, the predatory wolf became an enemy.

domesticated for their own use. When this happens, their image in human eyes changes: they are no longer considered admirable and courageous hunters but dangerous predators to be controlled or exterminated.

The change from a hunting and gathering way of life to one based on farming and herding began about 12,000 years ago, and since that time, wolves and humans have been on a collision course in many parts of the world. In Europe, forests were cut down during the Middle Ages to be replaced by farms and fields, and wolves lost their natural homes. Driven to seek prey in areas of human habitation, they attacked domestic animals and, on rare occasions, people. As the human population of Europe grew and wilderness areas disappeared, the conflict between wolves and humans became acute.

To rid themselves of this apparent threat to their lives and livelihoods, people set out to eliminate wolves from their territories. In most cases, they succeeded very well. By means of hunting with horses and dogs or trapping in pits and other devices, wolves were completely wiped out in England by the early 1500s. Scotland got rid of its last wolf in the mid-1700s. Other European countries took longer to do the job, but most eventually reached their goal.

Today there are only a few hundred wild wolves left in Western Europe, living in mountainous regions of Italy, Spain, Portugal, and the Scandinavian countries. Wolves are more common in Eastern Europe, and in the vast territory of Asia, particularly in the sparsely populated North, large numbers of the animals have survived human efforts to exterminate them.

Conflict between wolves and humans in the crowded countries of Western Europe was unavoidable, and people who believed they had to kill the predators in order to protect their own safety and well-being cannot be too harshly condemned for their actions. In this meeting between wolves and humans as in so many others, however, the human defenders seem to have been motivated by a special hatred of their animal adversaries. They saw wolves not as predatory animals behaving as nature meant them to but as evil creatures acting out of malice and viciousness.

This extreme attitude toward wolves can be seen in the fables and legends about the animals that originated in the Middle Ages and still survive today. Although a few traditional stories portrayed wolves as courageous or caring (Romulus and Remus, the twin founders of the city of Rome, were supposedly nursed by a kindly female wolf), most showed the animals as cunning, cruel, and bloodthirsty. The tale of Little Red Riding Hood is probably the most famous of these European fables of the Big, Bad Wolf, but there are many others.

In the Middle Ages, wolves were not only considered vicious but also thought to be in league with the forces of evil. Many legends connected the wolf with Satan and the dark powers of the supernatural world. This relationship was most clearly demonstrated in the activities of the so-called werewolves. A werewolf was a human who took on the form of a wolf by means of magic. In their animal forms, werewolves supposedly attacked people, killing and eating them.

Medieval Europe was not the only civilization that believed in werebeasts, people who take on the shape of animals. In different eras and in different parts of the world, there have been legends not only of werewolves but also of werefoxes, weretigers, wereleopards, and werejaguars. Only in Europe, however, were these legendary creatures associated so exclusively with the powers of evil and persecuted with such vigor and persistence. In the Middle Ages, hundreds of

A drawing from a medieval manuscript shows a werewolf grasping a human victim.

people were accused of the terrible crime of being werewolves. Some were brought to trial, convicted, and executed, usually by being burned alive.

Many of these so-called werewolves were probably mentally ill people whose strange behavior made them the objects of persecution in a superstitious age. They were treated with particular cruelty, however, because of their supposed association with that despised animal, the wolf. In this situation, the human prejudice against wolves caused people to treat other people with the ferocity they normally reserved for the predatory animals that they feared and hated.

When European settlers came to North America in the 1500s and 1600s, they found wolves inhabiting the deep forests and wide plains of the continent. In this vast new land, there might have been room for both human and animal predators to live their separate lives in peace. Instead, North America became the scene of the human race's most determined and successful campaign against the wolf.

Inspired by the traditional European hatred of the wolf, the early settlers attacked their enemy using pits, traps, and poison. They also employed bounties, cash rewards given by authorities to anyone who brought in the hide or some other part of a dead wolf. The American war against the wolf did not really get under way, however, until the 1800s, when people began to move onto the great plains in the center of the country. Here there were enormous herds of bison, which served as a food supply for Indian tribes and for large numbers of wolves. All three—Indian, bison, wolf— were doomed to be brought almost to the point of extinction by the relentless forces of "civilization."

At first, wolves were hunted for their thick winter fur, which brought a good price in European markets. Then as cattle and sheep grazing became common on the great open plains, the predators were killed because they preyed on the herds of domestic animals. (Their natural prey, the bison, had been greatly reduced in number by another human war against the animal world.)

The American *wolfers*, or wolf hunters, of the 19th century did not catch their prey with traps. Poison was more efficient and simpler to use. Strychnine, the favored poison of the wolfers, was placed in the carcasses of dead bison, cattle, or sheep. Wolves feeding on the animals would die, painfully, of strychnine poisoning. And so would any other creature— coyote, dog, bird, even human—that ate the poisoned flesh.

No one knows how many animals were killed during the last half of the 19th century, when the wolfers were most active in the western part of the United States. Perhaps 1 to 2 million wolves died, and thousands of other creatures fell victim to the wolfers' poisoned bait.

By 1900, there were not many wolves left in the western United States. The few remaining animals were still being pursued by wolfers, ranchers, and herders eager to eradicate the species completely from the American scene. In 1919, the federal government joined in the anti-wolf campaign, passing a law that called for the extermination of wolves on federally owned lands. By 1942 when the law was repealed, almost 25,000 wolves had been killed by government hunters.

In 1944, these wolves, along with several other predators, were shot from airplanes by bounty hunters in Minnesota.

This was the last phase of the organized campaign to rid the United States of the hated predator. By this time, the wolf had been virtually exterminated in most parts of the country. The situation remains almost unchanged today. In the lower 48 states, only Minnesota has a significant number of wolves—about 1,900 in the early 1990s. A few animals are also found in the states of Wisconsin, Michigan, and Montana. Remote Alaska has a substantial population of wolves, and the western provinces of Canada also harbor sizable numbers of the predators. Even in these areas, however, humans who hunt for pleasure frequently complain that wolves, hunting for food, cut down on the amount of prey available.

Today the wolf is classified as an endangered species in almost all parts of the United States except Minnesota and Alaska. This classification means that the killing of wolves is strictly controlled by federal law. For most wolves, such protection has come far too late. The killing has already taken place, and the millions of animals slaughtered in the past cannot be brought back to life. Ironically, most people now agree that the world is a poorer place because of their loss.

·8·
Wolf Pack

Tracking Wolves in the Wild

IN THE LATE 1930s, A BIOLOGIST NAMED ADOLPH MURIE began studying wolves in the vast territory of Mount McKinley National Park in Alaska. He spent almost three years following tracks left in the snow, searching for dens, watching wolf packs as they hunted or played. Since that time, many other scientists have conducted field research on the nature and habits of wolves. As a result of their work, we now have a great deal of information about the predators that past generations lacked. Thanks to these scientists, legends of the "big, bad wolf" have been replaced by facts about real wolves and their way of life.

L. David Mech, a biologist with the U. S. Fish and Wildlife Service, is an expert in the study of wolf behavior. Here he is imitating a wolf's howl to see if any wolves in the area will respond. The animals sometimes answer human howls and even come to see who or what is producing the noise.

To Catch a Wolf

Studying wolves in their natural environment is not an easy job. The animals are very wary, and they avoid humans as much as possible. In order to gain meaningful information about their behavior and habits, field researchers not only have to locate wolves in the wilderness but also have to observe the same individuals over a period of time. This requires being able to identify the animals in some way and to keep a record of them as they carry out the activities of their lives. In the following photographs, Dave Mech and another researcher, Holly Hertel, are shown using the techniques that have been developed to achieve these goals.

Catching a wolf is the first step in making it a useful part of a research project. Field researchers usually use a leg-hold trap that prevents the animal from escaping but does not injure it.

After trapping a wolf, the researcher gives the animal an injection of a drug that makes it unconscious (above). Then the wolf is given a thorough examination. It is measured and weighed (left).

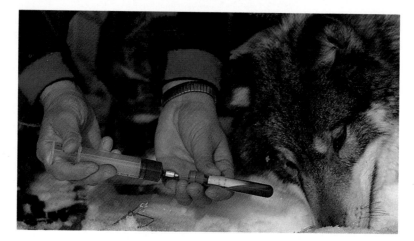

Blood samples are taken (above), and teeth are checked to learn the wolf's approximate age (below left). All these findings are carefully recorded.

The next step is to mark the wolf in some way so that it can be identified in the future. Attaching numbered tags to the animal's ear is one method of doing this (right). If the wolf is captured again, researchers will be able to check the record of the animal's previous history.

82·

Tracking Wolves by Radio

An even more practical way of identifying a trapped wolf
and making sure that it can be found again is to equip it
with a radio collar (above). This device, attached to the
animal's neck, contains a small battery-powered transmitter
that sends out a radio signal at a particular frequency.
Using receivers that pick up this signal, researchers can
locate the wolf after it is released and follow its movements.

Studying wolves that have been equipped with radio collars
has provided much useful information. Researchers like
David Mech and Holly Hertel have spent many months
tracking such animals in Minnesota's Superior National
Forest and other areas. They have learned about the territories that wolf packs occupy and the routes that they
travel. They have followed individual wolves through most
of the years of their lives, observing them in their daily
activities and examining them after death. Radio tracking
has become an invaluable tool for field research on wolves
and many other kinds of animals.

Holly Hertel checks the readings of an automatic radio-tracking monitor.

In order to track a wolf equipped with a radio collar, a researcher uses a receiver with an antenna that picks up the signal sent out by the collar's transmitter. Some receivers, like the one shown above, are stationary and operate automatically. They keep a record of the movements of collared animals within the range of their antennas.

Mobile receivers allow a researcher to go out and look for the animals that he or she is studying. Some animals can be tracked on foot, using a small receiver and a hand-held antenna, but with creatures as wide-ranging as wolves, an airplane is essential. Dave Mech and his colleagues in northern Minnesota use small planes with antennas attached to their wings to locate the collared wolves they are studying.

To locate an individual wolf, the pilot of the plane flies in circles above the area where the animal was last observed, while the field researcher listens through the radio receiver's earphones for the beeping signal sent out by the collar transmitter.

The researcher switches the receiver back and forth between the two antennas on the plane's wings, searching for signals that might be coming from either side of the plane.

When a signal is picked up, the pilot flies in the general direction of its source. The researcher continues to switch antennas, listening for the stronger signal in order to keep the plane on the right track. When the signals from both antennas are equally loud, the plane should be headed directly for the transmitting collar and the wolf. Once the wolf is located, information about its whereabouts and activities can be added to the field research records.

Researcher Holly Hertel is shown here transporting a drugged wolf in her backpack. In her hand she holds a capture collar, a useful piece of equipment that makes it possible to recapture a collared wolf.

A new and very useful development in the field of radio tracking is the capture collar, held by Holly Hertel in the picture on the opposite page. In addition to a transmitter, this kind of radio collar contains a receiver and two darts loaded with an anesthetizing drug. When a researcher wants to recapture a collared wolf, he or she radios a signal to the collar's receiver that releases one of the darts, injecting the wolf with the drug. If the first dart fails to act, the second one can be triggered as a backup. Following the signal of the collar's transmitter, the researcher can locate the unconscious wolf.

The capture collar solves one of the most difficult problems in conducting field research: how to get hold of an animal that has been captured once and is now roaming free. It is hard to trap a wolf a second or third time, but an animal equipped with a capture collar can be easily caught whenever the researcher wants to examine it. The collar also makes it easier to replace the batteries in the transmitter, which last for a limited amount of time. With the use of this unique piece of equipment, a research project can continue for many years.

Studying Captive Packs

Scientists working in the field have added greatly to our knowledge of wolves. Some aspects of wolf behavior, however, cannot be easily studied under field conditions. For example, an observer in an airplane will not be able to learn much about the complicated social relationships among members of a wolf pack. For this kind of research, scientists usually use captive wolves. By watching the day-to-day activities of a captive pack, a researcher is able to make a detailed record of the animals' behavior and the ways in which they communicate with each other.

Observing a captive wolf pup as it grows is a good way for a researcher to learn about a young wolf's development and habits. Here is Holly Hertel with a wolf pup that she raised as part of her research project.

Wolves raised in captivity often establish a close relationship with their human caretakers. They are never completely tame, however, and cannot be treated as pets. A wolf kept in a pen is as much a wild animal as one that roams the wilderness. Researchers hope that by studying a few wolves held in captivity, they can provide the information that will make it possible for most wolves to remain free.

Glossary

active submission—approaching a dominant wolf and licking or nipping its muzzle. Pack members often greet the alpha male in this manner.

alpha female—the female wolf at the top of a wolf pack's social structure

alpha male—the male wolf at the top of a wolf pack's social structure

beta male—the male wolf second in rank to the alpha male of a pack

cache (KASH)—a spot near a den where meat is buried for the use of a female wolf with pups

carnivores—animals that eat meat

color phases—the varying colors of pelage found within a group of wolves

courtship—a series of actions performed by animals in preparation for mating

den—an enclosure in which wolf pups are born and where they spend the first four weeks of their lives

digitigrade (DIJ-it-eh-grade)—walking on the digits, with the back part of the foot raised

dominance hierarchy (HI-er-ark-ee)—the social structure of a wolf pack, based on the positions of superiority and inferiority held by various pack members

dominant—holding a superior position over other members of the same group

guard hairs—the long outer hairs of a wolf's coat

litters—groups of pups born to a female wolf at one time. Most litters are made up of five to six pups.

pack—a group of wolves that live together, sharing the work of hunting and raising young

passive submission—a gesture in which a subordinate pack member lies on the ground and exposes its side or belly to a dominant wolf, expressing fear and inferiority

pelage (PEL-ij)—the hairy covering of a wolf's body

plantigrade (PLANT-eh-grade)—walking with the back part of the foot touching the ground

predators—animals that hunt and kill other animals for their food

raised-leg urination (RLU)—urinating with one hind leg raised. The dominant wolves in a pack make scent marks with RLUs.

regurgitate (ree-GUHR-jih-tate)—to bring up partially digested food from the stomach

rendezvous (RAHN-day-voo) site—a spot within a wolf pack's territory where pups are left when they are too young to join the pack in hunting

scent marking—using urine or other strong-smelling substances to mark the boundaries of a territory

scent post—a raised object such as a tree stump on which a wolf leaves a scent mark

territories—the areas in which wolf packs hunt and which they will defend from the intrusion of other packs

werewolf—a human who supposedly takes on the form of a wolf

wolfers—hunters who were hired to kill wolves in the United States during the last half of the 19th century

Index

ACKNOWLEDGMENTS

Photographs and illustrations courtesy of: pp. 2, 6, 18, 21, 42, 43, 44, 57, 60, 80, 81 (top), 82 (top), 83, 85, Layne Kennedy; pp. 10, 11, 13, 24, 29, 32, 37 (bottom), 39, 45, 47, 51, 56, 58, 62, 65, 90, Scot Stewart; pp. 12, 15, 16, Klaus Paysan; pp. 19, 25, 27, 28, 35, 37 (top), 38, 40, 49, 54, Janet Lidle; p. 31, Cheryl Asa; p. 71 (top), Museum of the American Indian; p. 72, British Museum; p. 77, Minnesota Department of Natural Resources; pp. 79, 81 (bottom), 82 (bottom left and right), 84, 86, 88, 89, Holly Hertel

Maps and diagrams based on material from: pp. 9, 63, *The Wolf: The Ecology and Behavior of an Endangered Species*, L. David Mech (University of Minnesota Press, 1970); p. 53, *Wolf and Man: Evolution in Parallel*, Roberta Hall and Henry Sharp, Editors (Academic Press, 1978); p. 85, *Handbook of Animal Tracking*, L. David Mech (University of Minnesota Press, 1983)

SYLVIA A. JOHNSON is a writer and editor who has published more than 20 books for young readers in the field of natural science. In addition to wolves, she has studied and written about such diverse forms of wildlife as penguins, silkworms, crabs, and snails. Her works have received awards from the National Science Teachers Association-Children's Book Council Joint Committee and from the New York Academy of Sciences.

ALICE AAMODT learned to understand and appreciate wolves through her work on an exhibit at the Science Museum of Minnesota entitled "Wolves and Humans: Coexistence, Competition and Conflict." As a member of the volunteer staff, she assisted the exhibit director in conducting research, creating an interpretative program, and training interpreters.